Dwadash Jyotirlingas

(Twelve Jyotirlingas)

Dr. Sarla Jagmohan

BOOKS FOR ALL
Delhi - 110052

Distributed by :
D. K. Publishers Distributors (P) Ltd.
1, Ansari Road, Darya Ganj,
New Delhi-110 002
Phones : 327 8368, 326 1465

ISBN 81-7386-216-8

Published by :
BOOKS FOR ALL
B-2, Vardhman Palace,
Nimri Commercial Centre,
Ashok Vihar Phase-IV,
Delhi-110 052
Phone : 740 1672

Laser Typeset by :
Steinmitz Electric Corporation
Hauz Khas, New Delhi-110016

Printed at :
D.K. Fine Art Press (P) Ltd.,
Delhi-110 052

PRINTED IN INDIA

Contents

1. Shri Somnath

This jyotirlinga is in the world- famous Somnath temple, situated by the seaside at Varaval in Kathiawar, Gujarat State. This region was originally known as Prabhas. It was here that Lord Krishna had done the leela of his life when struck by the arrow of a hunter called jara.

A fascinating legend can be found in Shiva Purana, according to which all the twenty-seven daughters of Daksha Prajapathi were married to Chandra, the Moon. However, the Moon had a special love for one of those daughters who was called Rohini. Daksha's other daughters were unhappy because of this preferential treatment of Rohini. When they complained about it to Daksha, he was so upset that he persuaded the Moon, but when Chandra did not heard, he curried Chandra so that it immediately fell victim to kshays and began to ware. With that, Chandra could no longer shower its cooling light on the earth.

Chandra was very unhappy and depressed. hearing his prayer, Indra and other gods and the sages like Vasistha went to Lord Brahma. After hearing everything, Brahma said, "You must go to Prabhas, the sacred Lord, along with other Gods and worship Lord Mrityunjaya (Shiva) there. By this grace, you would be certainly freed from your curse and from all illnesses."

Following that instruction, Chandra went to the sacred Lord of Prabhas where he worshipped Mrityunjaya. He performed a very hard penance, reciting the Mrityunjaya mantra ten crore times. Pleased with Chandra for his preserverence, Mrityunjaya granted him the boon of immortality. He said, "Oh, Chandra, do not grieve. Because of my boon, you would be free from your curse. At the same time, Prajapati Daksha's words would also be kept. During the dark fortnight of every month, you would lose one digit each day. But during the bright fortnight your digits would grow each day. Thus, on every Purnima, you would acquire your full form and you would shine in glory. "Everyone was happy because of this boon and there was joy in all the worlds. Chandra once again began showering his cooling bright light everywhere like before.

After becoming free from that curse Chandra, along with other Gods, prayed to Lord Mrityunjaya, "Lord, kindly grace this place by residing here for good with Mother Parvati for the redemption of all beings. Lord Shiva abided by Chandra's wish and started living there with Parvati in the form of the Jyotirlinga. It is situated in a cave under the sanctum sanatorum.

The greetness of this Jyotirlinga has been

mentioned in glorious terms in the Mahabharata, Shrimad Bhagavata, Skanda Purana, etc.

Chandra is also known as Soma, because he had worshipped Mrityunjaya as a supreme deity, this Jyotirlinga is known as Somnath. By worshiping this Jyotirlinga, the devotees are freed from all their sins and evil deeds of several births. They qualify themselves to win the grace and favour of Lord Shiva and Mother Parvati. The road to salvation automatically opens for them. All their action in this world and the other world bear fruits without effort.

mentioned in glorious terms in the Mahabharata, Shrimad Bhagavata, Skanda-Purana, etc.

Chandra is also known as Soma because he had worshipped Mrityunjaya as a supreme deity, this Jyotirlinga is known as Somnath. By worshipping this Jyotirlinga, the devotees are freed from all their sins and evil deeds of several births. They qualify themselves to win the grace and favour of Lord Shiva and Mother Parvati. The road to salvation automatically opens for them. All their action in this world and the other world bear fruits without effort.

2. Shri Mallikaarjuna

This Jyotirlinga is situated on the Shaila mountain on the back of the river Krishna in Andhra Pradesh. This mountain is called Mount Kailash of the South. It is said that a person becomes free from all miseries and is liberated from the cycle of birth and death by merely viewing the peak of that mountain. The greatness and significance of this Jyotirlinga have been described in detail in the Mahabharata, Shiva Purana, Padma Purana, etc.

As the legend goes Ganesh and Kartikeya, the two sons of Lord Shankara, quarrelled with each other. Both of them insisted on being married first. To settle that quarrel, Parvati said , "Who ever comes back early after going round the earth will be married first."

Hearing this, Kartikeya started at once to go round the earth. But it was difficult for Ganesha with his heavy body and only a little mouse as his vahana (vechicle). But his intelligence was very sharp. He thought of the easiest way of going round the earth. He paid the respects to his mother and father and completed his round of the earth by going round them seven times. This was in strict conformity with what was prescribed in the Shastras. " He who goes round the parents after duly worshiping them, gets without doubt the benefit of having gone round the earth."

By the time Kartikeya returned after making a full round of the earth. Ganesha had been already married to Siddhi and Buddhi and had two sons called Kshema and Labha. When Kartikeya saw that Ganesh was married before him and also had two sons, he was very much offended and went off to the Krouncha mountain.

Mother Parvati went to the Krauncha mountain to pacify Kartikeya. She was followed by Lord Shankara who revealed himself in the form of the Jyotirlinga. That Jyotirlinga came to be known as Mallikarjuna because it was first worshipped with the offering of mallika flowers.

According to another legend, King Chandragupta had his capital near this Shaila mountain. His daughter left the palace to protect herself from a particular calamity and started living with the cowherds. That Princes had a beautiful black cow. Somebody secretly milched her everyday. One day, that Princess accidentally caught the person in the act. Furiously, she rushed towards that thief. But as she went up to the cow , she saw nothing there except a Shivalinga.

Some time later, that princess built a grand temple over that Shivalinga, which came to be known as

Mallikarjuna. Every year on Shivaratri day, there is a big fair.

The Mallikarjuna Shivalinga has been described with all its greatness and glory in the Puranas. It is said that when people visit this sacred place and worship this Shivalinga with devotion, their good desires are fulfilled and they become completely devoted to Lord Shiva. They become free from all obstructions. Their dedication to Lord Shiva takes them along the path of salvation.

3. Shri Mahakaleshwara

This sacred Jyotirlinga is situated at the city of Ujjain in Madhya Pradesh. In ancient times, this city on the bank of the Kshipra river, was known as Ujjayini and also as Avantikapuri. It is one of the seven sacred cities of India.

According to the legend in the Puranas, King Chandrasena ruled the city of Ujjayini in ancient times. He was a devout worshipper of Lord Shiva. One day , a five year old cowherd boy was passing from there with his mother. He was wonder struck and curious when he saw the King worshipping Lord Shiva. He also felt inspired to worship Lord Shiva in the same manner. However, he would not gather the necessary items to do the puja. Therefore on his way back home, he picked up a stone from the road. After coming to the house, he installed that stone as a Shivalinga and started worshipping it with great devotion with flowers, sandal paste, etc. His mother came to call him for meal. But he was not prepared to get up, leaving his worship half way. His mother was so furious that she picked up that stone and flung it far away, The boy was very upset and started crying, calling and name of Lord Shiva. He continued to cry and ultimately dropped there unconscious.

Lord Shiva, deeply moved by this boy's devotion, was greatly pleased. As the boy regained his consciousness and opened his eyes, he found before him a grand golden temple, studded with gems. In that temple was an extremely brilliant and shining Jyotirlinga. The boy overwhelmed with joy and happiness, started singing praises of Lord Shiva.

When his mother got this information, she rushed to him and pressed her dear son to her heart. Soon after, king Chandrasena also came there and praised the boy for what he had achieved. In no time, a big crowd collected there.

In the meantime, Hanumana appeared on the scene and said, "Oh, ye human beings, Lord Shiva is the first among the gods that brings you quick results. Appeased by the devotion of this child, Lord Shiva has given him such a great reward which the great sages cannot have ever through the penance in millions of births. A cowherd called Nanda would be born in the eight generation of this boy. In the Dwapara Yuga, Vishnu would be born as Krishna in his house where he would have all kinds of Leelas." After saying this, Hanumana vanished. Shrikara and king Chandrasena continued worshipped Lord Shiva and ultimately went to the abode of the Lord.

There is another legend about this Jyotirlinga. According to this legend, there lived in Avantikapuri, an extremely brilliant Brahmin. He was given to doing hard penance and was well-versed in the Vedas. One day, a tyrant demon called Dushana came there to create obstacles in his penance. He had acquired tremendous powers because of the boon he had received from Brahma. Seeing that the Brahmin was in trouble, Lord Shiva who showers beneficence to all living beings, appeared. With a single angry shout, he burned that tyrant demon to ashes. With another angry cry, the Lord appeared on the spot. That is how Lord Shiva came to be as Mahakala, and this sacred Jyotirlinga is called Mahakala. Its glory has been described in detail in the Mahabharata, Shiva Purana and Skanda Purana.

This is a very huge Shivalinga. In the silver water-casket is a Naga. The idols of Ganesha is on one side, of Parvati on the second side and of Kartikeya is the third side. In front of the door is the idol of Nandi. Huge crowds gather at this place on Shivaratri day. And the Kumbha-mela on the bank of the Kshirpa river is very famous.

4. Shri Omkareshwara, Shri Amaleshwara

This jyotirlinga is situated in Madhya Pradesh on the bank of the sacred Narmada river. The river flows into two currents at this spot and it has created an island which is known as the Mandhata parvat or Shivpuri. One current of the river flows to the north of the island and the other flows to the south. The current flowing southward is considered the main current of the river. It is on the Mandhata Parvat that the Jyotirlinga of Shri Omkareshwara is situated.

One has to pass through two small rooms to reach the temple of this Jyotirlinga. Since there is darkness inside the temple, lamps are kept burning day and night.

The Jyotirlinga of Shri Omkareshwara has not bear created by human hands. It is the creation of nature itself. There is always water around that Shivalinga. The entire Mandhata Parvat itself is said to be the manifestation of Shiva. That is why that place is also known as Shivapuri. Devout worshippers circumbilate round this Shivalinga.

A very big fair is organised there on the Kartiki Purnima day. People offer **channa daal** to the Shivalinga. the arati for putting the god to sleep is a grand affair.

The Omkareshwara Jyotirlinga has two forms, one of which is known as Amaleshwara. This Shivalinga is on the southern bank of the Narmada river, a little far from Omkareshwara. But though separate, they are considered one.

The legend pertaining to the two forms of this Shivalinga is as follows :

According to the Puranas, the Vindhya mountain, once did hard penance for six months to worship Lord Shiva in the manner of the mortals. Pleased by that worship, Lord Shiva appeared in that spot and granted several boons to fulfill the wishes of the Vindhya mountain.

A large number of sages arrived there when the Vindhya mountain was granted the boons. At their request Shiva divided the Linga into two parts. In one part he entered in the form of Pranva (Omkar) and it came to be known as Omkareshvara. The other part, that embodied the earthly Linga, came to be known as Amareshwara or Amaleshwara. These Lingas and their temples are separate, but they are regarded as one.

Shiva Purana contains the detailed description of the greatness of this Jyotirlinga. While indicating the merit one would earn by the **darshan** of Shri Omkareshwara and Shri Amaleshwara, the sacred reward of bathing in the Narmada is also mentioned. Everyone should go for the darshan of this Jyotirlinga because it brings the highest rewards of this world and also the other world. For such a one, the means of arth, dharma, karma and moksha become easily available.

Lord Shiva shower grace on the devotees for no reason at all. He is a supreme giver. What then to say about the good fortune of those, who come for his **darshan**? For them, the gates of the highest merit open for all times to come.

5. Shri Kedareshwara or Shri Kedarnath

The shrine of Kedarnatha or Kedareshwara is situated on the Kedara peak of the Himalaya, in the midst of breath-taking sylvan beauty. On its east flows the Alaknanda river where we have the world famous Badrinath temple. On the west in the Mandakini river with the Kedareshwara temple on its bank. These two rivers, as they flow down, and mingling together, for the sacred Bhagirathi Ganga at Devaprayag. Thus, the devotees who bathe in the sacred Ganga river touch the waters that have washed the feet of Shri Kedareshwara and Badrinatha.

The Jyotirling of Kedarnatha is about 150 miles from Haridwar and 132 miles from Rishikesh.

According to the legend in the Puranas, the great ascetic Shrinara and Narayana had performed hard penance for several years to propitiate Lord Shiva on the lovely Kedar peek of the Himalaya. For thousands of years, they worshipped Lord Shiva, without taking food and standing on one leg. People everywhere talked with admiration about their penance. The gods, sages,

Yakshas and Gandharvas praised their sadhana and their self-restraint. Even Brahma, the creator and Vishnu, the protector were all praises for this penance of Nar-Narayana. Finally Lord Shiva, the giver of great boons, also was moved by their penance and appeared before them in person. The two sages, overwhelmed by appearance of Lord Shiva, started singing glory of the Lord by reciting hymns of various kinds and worshipped him. When Lord Shiva wanted to grant boons to them they said, "Oh, you greatest among the gods, Mahadev, if you are really pleased with our penance, kindly install yourself in this place for ever for the benefit of your devotees. Thereby this place will become sanctified and people will come here to worship you with all devotion."

Hearing the request of the sages, Lord Shiva installed himself there in the form of a Jyotirlinga. It came to be known as shri Kedarnatha (Kedareshwara) Jyotirlinga because it was installed on the Kedar peek of the Himalaya.

In the Satya yuga, Upamanyu had worshipped Lord Shiva here. In the Dwapara yuga, the Pandavas also had worshipped the Lord in this very place.

The Puranas and the scriptures refer to this Jyotirlinga in glorious terms. All through the ages, the devotees have been worshipping this Jyotirlinga for the fulfillment of their wishes in this life and in the end, to attain **moksha** or salvation.

6. Shri Bhimeshwara or Shri Bhimshankara

This Jyotirlinga is situated on the Brahmapura mountain range near Guwahati on the bank of the Bhima river.

A legend in the Shiva Purana describes this Jyotirlinga as follows :

In ancient times, there was a powerful demon called Bhim who live in Kamaroop with his mother. This demon was the son of Kumbhakarna, broter of the demon king Ravana, but he had never seen his father. When he was still a child, Kumbhakarna had been killed by Lord Rama. When he entered youth, his mother told him how his father had been killed by Rama, who was the incarnation of Lord Vishnu, he was beside himself with rage. He was obsessed with the thought of avenging his father's death at the hands of Rama. He performed hard penance for a thousand years to attain his objective. Pleased by his penance, Lord Brahma gave him a boon that he would become a world conqueror. After that, by the grace of Brahmaji, that demon started harassing all living beings. He even attached the abode of the gods and drove them away from there, and established his own power there. Then he defeated Shri Hari in a battle. Later, he attacked king Sudakshin of Kamaroop who was a devoted worshipper of Lord Shiva and imprisoned him along with his ministers and attendants. That way, he became the master of all the three worlds, that spelled all round destruction. Even the Vedas, Puranas and the scriptures as well. He did not allow anyone to do any religious act.

Scared by the terror he was letting loose everywhere, the sages and the gods went to Lord Shiva for protection. They narrated Lord Shiva all the Lordships they themselves and other living beings had listening to their appeal; Lord Shiva said, "Very soon I shall slay that demon. He does not deserve to live after he made my devotee king Sudakshina and his attendants captive."

On the other hand, king Sudakshina worshipped Lord Shiva in his captivity, with a Shivalinga in front. The enraged demon Bhima stuck that Shivalinga with his sword. But the sword had hardly touched the Linga and Lord Shiva emerged in person from it and with a loud cry reduced that demon into ashes.

All the sages and all the gods immediately started singing the glory of Lord Shiva. They urged him to make that place his permanent abode for the welfare of the people and sanctify it thereby. Lord Shiva, abiding by that request resided in that Linga for god which came to be known as the Bhimeshwar Jyotirlinga.

This legend is narrated in detail in the Shiva Purana (chapters 19 to 21). The wishes of the devotees who come to worship this Jyotirlinga are fulfilled.

7. Shri Vishweshwara

This Jyotirlinga has been installed at India's reputed city Kashi under the name of Vishwanath. According to the scriptures, this city remains safe even in the midst of a deluge, because at such a critical moment, Lord Shiva holds it aloft on his trident, and sets it down in its place again at the time of creation. This city has also been called the original city of the universe. It is said that it was here that Lord Vishnu, inspired by his desire for creation, had performed penance to propitiate Lord Shiva. Sage Agastya also had performed penance in the same place to please Lord Shiva. The great significance of this city is such that anyone who abandons his bay body here, attains **moksha** and is freed from the cycle of birth and death. It has been said, "Even a person sunk deep in the pleasures of the senses and absolutely averse to religion, attains freedom from the bondages of worldly life if he dies in the sacred city of Kashi." In the Matsya purana, it has been said about Kashi, "Kashi is the only place of salvation for those human beings who have lived without reciting God's name and doing meditation and acquired no knowledge and who are afflicted by miseries and unhappiness.

To the west of this sacred city, is Omkarakhanda, to the south is Kedarkhanda and in the middle is Vishweshwarakhanda where the world famous Vishweshwara Jyotirlinga has been installed.

The Puranas narrate the following legend about this Jyotirlinga :

Lord Shiva had been living on the Kailash mountain after his marriage with Parvati. But Parvati did not like living in the father's house after marriage. She complained that while girls always went to live in their husband's houses, she was compelled to live in her father's house. She urged Lord Shiva to take her to this house. Lord Shiva, abiding by Parvati's request, came with her to the sacred city of Kashi and installed himself there in the form of the Jyotirlinga.

The original Jyotirlinga of Shri Vishwanath is not available, as the original temple had been destroyed by the Mughal Emperor Aurangzeb. It is said that the original idol is lying in the Jnanavati. The new Vishwanatha temple was built by Ahilya Bai, the Maharani of Indore, who was a devout worshipper of Lord Shiva. Swami Karapatri also built a Vishwnatha temple close to the river Ganga where people can worship and offer their prayers from a distance.

Those who worship the Vishweshwara Jyotirlinga are freed from all their sins and Lord Shiva always showers his grace on them.

8. Shri Tryambakeshwara

This Juotirlinga is situated at Nasik in the Maharashtra state on the bank of Godavari river which is considered as sacred as the Ganga.

According to the legend in the Shiva Purana, the wives of the Brahmins living in the **tapovan** of the great sage Gautama were offended with his wife Ahalya. They instigated their husbands to do something to harm Gautama. They worshipped Lord Ganesha. When pleased by the worship of those Brahmins, Lord Ganesha wanted to give them a boon they said, "Oh, Lord, if you are really pleased with us, please drive the sage Gautama out of this ashram." Lord Ganesha urged them not ask such a boon, but they were adamant. In the end, Lord Ganesha had to give in. To abide by the wishes of his devotees, he assumed the form of a sickly cow and started grazing in a field which belonged to the sage Gautama.

Finding that cow grazing in his field, sage Gautama went up to the cow and very gestly tried to drive it away with a blade of grass. At the very touch of that grass the cow fell dead on the spot. This led to a tremendous uproar. All the Brahmins gathered there and describing sage Gautama as a cow-killer, condemned him in the strongest terms.

Sage Gautama, astonished by what had happened, felt miserable. The Brahmins insisted that he should immediately leave the ashram and go to live elsewhere. They said that they would incur sin by living with someone who had killed a cow. Sage Gautama, out of helplessness, left the ashram with his wife Ahalya. He started living in a place a little away from that ashram. But the Brahmins pursued him even there and made things very difficult for him. They said, "By killing a cow, you have forfeited the right to read the Vedas or perform any religions rites."

With utmost politeness, sage Gautama requested them to show him the way for expiation and redemption. The Brahmins said, "Gautama, you must go round the whole earth there times, proclaiming every where that you have committed the sin of killing a cow. After you return here, you must observe a fast for one month. At the end of that fast, you must go round the Brahmagiri mountain 101 times after which you will become pure. Otherwise, bring down the Ganga river here and after bathing with that water, bathe one crore Shivalingas to worship Lord Shiva, after which you must bathe again with water of the Ganga and go round the Brahmagiri mountain 11 time. Then you must bathe the Shivalinga with 100 pot of of the sacred water. With that you will be redeemed of you sin."

Sage Gautama did everything that those Brahmins wanted him to do and then, along with his wife, started worshipping Lord Shiva with complete and single-minded devotion. Lord Shiva was extremely pleased with the devoted worship by sage Gautama and appearing before him in person, urged him to ask for a boon. Sage Gautama said, "Oh, Lord, all I want is to be redeemed from the sin of killing a cow."

Lord Shiva said, "Gautama, you have always been without any blemish and have committed no sin. You were tricked into killing that cow. I want to punish those Brahmins for their foul act."

Gautama said, "Oh Lord! It in only because of them that I am privileged to have you darshan. Consider their action as the greatest good they did to me and do not get angry with them. A large number of sages and gods gathered there to support sage Gautama. They requested Lord Shiva to reside in that place for good. Lord Shiva agreed to that request and lived there in what came to be known as the Trymbakeshwara Jyotirlinga which grants all the merits to the devotees. The Ganga which sage Gautama had brought down there started floating nearby as the river Godavari (Gautami Ganga). When Brihaspati comes in the Sinha Rashi, a very big Kumbhamela is held there. Large number of devotees attend the Kumbhamela and purify themselves by bathing in the Godavari river and worshipping this Jyotirlinga.

9. Shri Vaidyanatha

This Jyotirlinga is situated in the Santhal Pargana of Bihar. This place, known as Vaidyanatha Dham, is at Deodhar, 100 kms. South-east of the Kiul railway station on the Patna-Calcutta railway track.

The legend about the establishment of this Jyotirlinga is as follows :

Ravana, the demon king, once performed a very hard penance in the Himalaya to propitiate Lord Shiva. He severed his ten leads one by one and offered them to the Shivalinga, he offered his nine heads that way. When he was about to cut his tenth head, Lord Shiva, extremely pleased and satisfied, appeared before Ravana in person. Holding back Ravana's hand before he would cut his tenth head. Lord Shiva restored his nine heads in their places and wanted to greet him a boon.

As a boon, Ravana sought Lord Shiva's permission to take that Shivalinga to Lanka, his capital. Lord Shiva did grant him that boon, but made condition : "You can certainly take it with you. But on the way, if you put it down anywhere, it would get firmly installed in that same place and you would not be able to move it."

Ravana agreed to that condition. Lifting that Shivalinga, he set out on his return journey to Lanka. On the way, it became very necessary for him to pass urine at one place. Handing over the Shivalinga to an Ahir. He went to relieve himself .

In the meantime, that Ahir found the weight of the Shivalinga too heavy. He could not hold it. Out of helplessness, he placed the Shivalinga right there on the ground. When Ravana came back, he tried his utmost to lift the Shivalinga from the ground. But it was all in vain. Ultimately, when all his efforts failed, he left that Shivalinga just there imprinting on it his thumb mark and returned to Lanka.

Subsequently, Brahma, Vishnu and other gods came to that spot and worshipped that Shivalinga. After installing that Shivalinga there, they returned to their respective abodes. This is the Jyotirlinga which is well known by the name of Vaidyanatha.

This Vaidyanatha Jyotirlinga grants infinite grace on the devotees. It is eleven angula (finger's breadth) high, on the tip of which is a dert in the shape of a thumb. It is said that is the mark, Ravana had imprinted with his thumb.

It is customary to anoint this Shivalinga with the water brought from distant sacred places. This

Jyotirlinga is very famous for freeing the devotees from all diseases. It is said in the Puranas that the man who has the darshan of this Jyotirlinga is redeemed from all his sins. Lord Shiva always showers his grace on him. He is never troubled by any physical afflictions, wrath of the gods or any earthly hardships. By the grace of Lord Shiva, he is free from all obstruction, diseases and sorrows. And he finds his place in the peaceful and quiet abode of Lord Shiva. He sees only Lord Shiva everywhere in the world. He has tender feeling of affection and kindness for all living creatures. He makes no distinction among them. He has no feeling of jealousy, malice, vengeance, hatred or anger towards any living creature. Such a devotee always works for the welfare and good of everyone.

People come from far and near to anoint this Jyotirlinga with sacred water. The devotees make this pilgrimage carrying **kanwar** on their shoulders and all the merits due to them for their dedicated worship.

10. Shri Nageshwara

This Jyotirlinga is situated in a spot nearly 17 miles from Dwarka in the Gujarat state.

The Puranas give the following legend about this Jyotirlinga :

There was a Vaishya called Supriya who was a deeply religious and righteous man. He was a great devotee of Lord Shiva. He spent his time worshipping Lord Shiva with complete devotion. With his thought, word and deed, he was always deep in the worship of Lord Shiva.

There was a demon named Daruk who found Supriya's devotion to Lord Shiva very irksome. It enraged him beyond control. He persistently tried in so many ways to cause obstructions in his worship of Lord Shiva.

One day, Supriya was going somewhere in a boat. The demon Daruk thought it was a good opportunity for him to destroy Supriya. He attacked that boat and making all the passengers captive, took them to his capital.

Supriya continued worshipping Lord Shiva even in prison as usual. Not only that, he also inspired other prisoners to do the same. When Daruk heard about this from his attendants, he was beside himself with rage and rushed to the prison with thumping steps. Supriya was seated at that time with his eyes closed, deeply in meditation at the feet of Lord Shiva.

Finding Supriya in that posture, Daruk thundered in a terrifying voice, "Oh, you devil Vaishya! What conspiracy are you hatching to create some trouble, sitting there with your eyes closed?" In spite of that menacing threat, the meditation of that devotee of Shiva was not broken.

Fretting and fuming, the demon Daruk ordered his attendants to kill not only Supriya but all other prisoners as well. But Supriya was not perturbed in the least by that order of Daruk. With supreme concentration and devotion, he called out Lord Shiva to free him and other prisoners from the clutches of that demon. He was absolutely certain that Lord Shiva whom he had worshipped with unflinching devotion, would free all of them from prison.

Hearing Supriya's prayer, Lord Shiva instantly appeared in the prison in the form of a Jyotirlinga shining bright at some height, seated on a throne. Thus appearing before Supriya, Lord Shiv also give him a Pashupat weapon. Supriya after killing Daruk and his companions with that weapon, went to live in the abode of Lord Shiva. Following the command of Lord Shiva himself, this Jyotirlinga was named Nageshwara.

The scriptures have written about the glory of this Jyotirlinga in glowing terms. It said that anyone who listens in good faith the story of the origin and greatness of this Jyotirlinga, is freed from all sins and after experiencing all kind of happiness, ultimately entitles himself to go to the abode of Lord Shiva.

It is said that at the time of the emergence of this Jyotirlinga, a lovely temple with four entrances also came up with that Jyotirlinga shining in the centre. This Jyotirlinga came to be known as Nageshwara and Parvati, who had also appeared there in person at that time, came to be called Nageshwari. All those who listen to this story and worship Nageshwara and Nageshwari with devotion, are redeemed from their sins and after experiencing wordly happiness, attain the state of **moksha**.

11. Shri Setubandh Rameshwara

This Jyotirlinga has been installed by Shri Ramachandra who is known as **Maryada Purshottama,** the ruler who was wedded to proper and dignified conduct. The legend about this Jyotirlinga is as follows :–

When Shri Ramachandra was on his way to invade Lanka, he had shaped this Shivalinga with the sand on this seashore and worshipped it. It is also said that sitting in that place, Shri Rama was drinking water when there was as oracle : "Are you taking water without worshipping me? Hearing those words, Shri Rama made a Shivalinga with the sand and worshipping it, asked for boon that he should conquer Ravana. Lord Shiva very happily granted that boon to Shri Rama. For the welfare of the people, Lord Shiva settled down there in the form of that Shivalinga and accepted all the prayers that were offered there since that time, this Jyotirlinga has been existing there.

There in also another legend about this Jyotirlinga. According to this legend, Shri Rama was returning after slaying Ravana and he had his first camp this side of the sea on the Gandhamadana mountain. A large number of rishis and munis came there to have his **darshan**. Shri Rama, while welcoming and greeting all of them he said that slaying Ravana who was the descendant of the Palasyta dynasty, he has incurred the sin of Brahmahatya. He urged then to show a way of redeeming himself from that sin.

Hearing that, the rishis and the munis who had gathered there said that he should install a Shivalinga there and thereby, free himself from that sin.

Shri Rama accepted that suggestion and ordered Hanumana to go to the Kailash mountain and bring a Shivalinga from there. Hanumnaa went to the Kailash mountain at once, but he could not see Lord Shiva there. Therefore, Hanumana sat down right there and performed the penance. After some time, he could have the darshan of Lord Shiva and came back with a Shivalinga. But fearing the auspicious hour would have passed by that time, Sita had already installed a Shivalinga there.

Hanumana was greatly distressed to see what had happened. He narrated his anguish to Shri Rama who explained to him the reason for installing the Shivalinga before his return. He said, he could remove the Shivalinga which had been installed earlier. Hanumana was very happy and immediate started digging that

Shivalinga. But Hanumana could not move that Shivalinga even slightly. Ultimately, he tried to remove that Shivalinga by winding his tail round it. But the Shivalinga still did not move. On the contrary, Hanuman was pushed and flung far away. He became unconscious and his body started bleeding. Everyone around was deeply pained to see Hanumana bleeding. Sita who loved Hanumana more than a son, started stroking his body and wailing. When he was out of his swoon, he saw Shri Rama before him in the form of the Supreme Brahma. Shri Rama explained to Hanumana the greatness of Lord Shiva and enlightened him. The Linga brought by Hanumana was installed near by. The Skanda Purana explains in detail the greatness of this Linga. This Shivalinga came to be called Hanumadiswara.

The Rameshwara temple is very big and grand. Apart from the great Shivalinga, there are many other images of Lord Shiva and other deities. Abount 20 miles from the Rameshwara temple, there is a place for pilgrimage called Dhanushkoti which is visited for performing **shraddha** and other religious rites.

12. Shri Ghushmeshwara

The last among the twelve Jyotirlingas is Ghushmeshwara or Ghrishneshwara. It is situated near a village called Verul in Maharashtra, twelve miles from Daulatabad.

The legend about this Jyotirlinga found in the Puranas is as follows :

A very pious Brahmin lived near the Devagiri mountain in the south. His name was Sudharma and his wife's name was Sudeha. Sudharma used to perform hard penance.

Sudharma and Sudeha loved each other very deeply. There was cause to make them unhappy, except that they had no children. According to astrological calculations Sudeha was not fated to bear children. Sudeha yearned to have children in the house. He urged Sudharma to have another marriage. She suggested his marriage with her younger sister.

At first that great Brahmin did not react favourably to his wife's suggestion. But in the end, he had to abide by her wish. He married her younger sister

Ghusma and brought her home. Ghushma was a very polite and righteous woman. She was a great devotee of Lord Shiva. She made one hundred earthly Shivalinga every day and worshipped them with heart-felt devotion. By the grace of Lord Shiva, in a short time, she gave birth to a lovely and healthy son. Both sudeha and Ghushma were happy beyond words at the birth of that child.

The two sisters lived happily and in harmony. But some time later, Sudeha was seized by an evil thought. She started feeling, "Nothing in this house belongs to me. Everything was in Ghushama's possession. She has established her authority over my husband. The child also belongs to Ghushma.

Gradually, that evil thought become on obsession with her . In the meantime Ghushma's son was also growing up. In course of time, he become a young man and was married. By that time Sudeha's evil thought had turned like a sprout grown into a huge tree, One day, she killed Ghushama's son, who was in the prime of youth, in sleep. She threw the dead body in the same pond in which Ghushma used to throw the Shivalingas everyday.

When this fact came to light in the morning, the whole house came under the shadow of gloom. It was filled with loud wailing. Sudharma and his daughter-in-law banged their heads and wept inconsolably. But

Ghushma was absorbed as usual in worshipping Lord Shiva. She continued praying as though nothing had happened, after completing her routine worship, she went to that pond to dump the Shivalinga in the water of that pond. As she was about to return from the pond, she found her darling son emerging from the pond and walking towards her. As usual, he came and fell at Ghushma's feet. It was as though he had returned after having a leisurely walk nearly. Right at that moment. Lord Shiva appeared and urged Ghushma to ask for a boon. He was furious with Sudaha on account of her hateful deed. He was impatient to strike her with this trident, thrusting it through her neck. But Ghushma pleaded him with folded hands, "Oh, Lord, if you are really pleased with me, kindly forgive my unfortunate sister. She has no doubt committed the most contemptible sin. But by your grace, I have got back my son. Now you do forgive her. And grant me one more thing. Kindly settle down here for good for the benefit of the people at large.

Lord Shiva granted both her wishes and settled down there in the form of a Jyotirlinga. In view of the unflinching devotion of Ghushma, came to be known as Ghushmeshwara Mahadev.

The greatness of Ghushmeshwara Jyotirlinga has been written about in glowing terms in the Puranas. The darshan of this Jyotirlinga brings good rewards in this world as well as the other world.

SHRI SOMNATH

SHRI MALLIKAARJUN

SHRI MAHAKALESHWARA

SHRI OMKARESHWARA

SHRI KEDARESWARA

SHRI BHIMESHWARA

SHRI VISHVESHWARA

SHRI TRYAMBAKESHWARA

SHRI VAIDYANATH

SHRI NAGESHWARA

SHRI SETUBANDH RAMESHWARA

SHRI GHUSHMESHWAR